DISCOVERY IN SONG

DISCOVERY IN SONG

Robert Heyer, S.J.
Thomas O'Brien
Thomas Sheehan
Patrick Collins
William Weber
Designed by **Emil Antonucci**
Photographed by **Ken Wittenberg**
Discovery Series Director: **Richard Payne**

PAULIST PRESS
Paramus, N.J. / New York, N.Y.

NOTE: The lyrics of certain songs are not included in *Discovery in Song* due to the refusal of reprint permission by the copyright owners. It was the decision of the authors to retain these songs along with the teen viewpoints, questions and photographs. The authors believe these songs to be essential to any comprehensive treatment of contemporary popular music. They suggest that an audit of the recording by the group or class combined with the material provided in the book will suffice for effective discussion.

CONTENTS

Introduction 9

Theme of Communication: "Shells Upon The Shore"
Introduction 15
She's Leaving Home *by Lennon & McCartney (Beatles)* **16**
Nowhere Man *by Lennon & McCartney (Beatles)* **19**
Sounds of Silence *by Paul Simon (Simon and Garfunkel)* **21**
Little Boxes *by Malvina Reynolds (Pete Seeger)* **23**
Penny Lane *by Lennon & McCartney (Beatles)* **24**
I Think It's Going To Rain Today *by Newman (Judy Collins)* **26**
The Dangling Conversation *by Paul Simon (Simon & Garfunkel)* **28**
The Flower Lady *by Phil Ochs (Jim and Jean)* **30**
People *by Styne and Merrill (Barbra Streisand)* **33**
What A Great Thing It Is *by Ray Repp (Ray Repp)* **35**
Appendix 36

Theme of Freedom: "Tear Down The Walls"
Introduction 39
Patterns *by Paul Simon (Simon & Garfunkel)* **41**
I Wanna Be Free *by Boyce and Hart (The Monkees)* **42**
Little Wheel Spin and Spin *by Buffy Sainte-Marie (Same)* **45**
Born Free *by Barry and Black (R. Williams)* **47**
Links On A Chain *by Phil Ochs (Phil Ochs)* **48**
Society's Child *by Janis Ian (Janis Ian)* **51**
Now That The Buffaloe's Gone *by Buffy Sainte-Marie (Same)* **53**
The Lonesome Death of Hattie Carroll *by Bob Dylan (Same)* **55**
Power and Glory *by Phil Ochs (Phil Ochs)* **56**
The Times They Are A-Changin' *by Bob Dylan (Bob Dylan)* **59**
Appendix **60**

Theme of Love: "Oaks and Willows"
Introduction 63
Eleanor Rigby *by Lennon and McCartney (Beatles)* **64**
Hair of Spun Gold *by Janis Ian (Janis Ian)* **67**
Within You Without You *by Lennon & McCartney (Beatles)* **68**
Alfie *by Bacharach and David (Dionne Warwick)* **71**
I'm A Believer *by Neil Diamond (The Monkees)* **72**
Sittin' On A Fence *by Jagger & Richard (Rolling Stones)* **75**
Georgy Girl *by Springfield & Dale (The Seekers)* **76**
If I Fell *by Lennon & McCartney (Beatles)* **78**
Crucifixion *by Phil Ochs (Jim and Jean)* **80**
God Is Love *by C. J. Rivers (C. J. Rivers)* **84**
Appendix **86**

Theme of Happiness: "Smiling Faces I Can See"
Introduction 89

Satisfaction *by Jagger & Richard* (*Rolling Stones*) **91**
Over Under Sideways Down *by The Yardbirds* (*Yardbirds*) **93**
Satisfied Kind *by Rhodes & Hayes* (*Joan Baez*) **94**
As Tears Go By *by Jagger & Richard & Oldham* (*Rolling Stones*) **97**
Getting Better *by Lennon & McCartney* (*Beatles*) **99**
Mother's Little Helper *by Jagger & Richard* (*Rolling Stones*) **100**
Mrs. McKenzie *by Janis Ian* (*Janis Ian*) **103**
Bottle of Wine *by Tom Paxton* (*Tom Paxton*) **105**
Appendix **106**

Theme of Peace: "When Will They Ever Learn"
Introduction **109**
Last Night I Had The Strangest Dream *by McCurdy* (*Pete Seeger*) **110**
Eve Of Destruction *by Sloan* (*Barry McGuire*) **113**
What Have They Done To The Rain *by Reynolds* (*Joan Baez*) **115**
The Universal Soldier *by Buffy Ste-Marie* (*Buffy Ste-Marie*) **116**
Masters of War *by Bob Dylan* (*Bob Dylan*) **118**
I Ain't Marchin' Any More *by Phil Ochs* (*Phil Ochs*) **121**
Blowin' In The Wind *by Bob Dylan* (*Peter, Paul & Mary*) **123**
Appendix **124**

Theme of Life: "One Last Cup Of Wine"
Introduction **127**
Flowers Never Bend In The Rainfall *by Simon* (*Simon & Garfunkel*) **129**
Five O'Clock World *by Reynolds* (*Vogues*) **130**
A Day In The Life *by Lennon & McCartney* (*Beatles*) **133**
Changes *by Phil Ochs* (*Phil Ochs*) **135**
Circle Game *by Joni Mitchell* (*Buffy Sainte-Marie*) **136**
Appendix **138**

Introduction

"We're more popular than Jesus Christ now. . . . Jesus was all right but his disciples were thick and ordinary. It's them twisting it that ruins it for me."

This statement was made by John Lennon of the Beatles in the summer of 1966. In its wake there came a new wave of public and private protest against the popular British group. Disc jockeys refused to play their recordings on the air. Both city hall and pulpit warned that the Beatles were dangerous for the morals of American youth. On the contrary, Thurston N. Davis, S.J., editor of *America* magazine, wrote: ". . . it seems to me that Lennon was merely stating what many a Christian educator would readily admit—that Christianity must come alive again in the minds and hearts of the young." (*America* Aug 20 '66)

Is John Lennon more popular than Jesus Christ? What does religion mean to the people incensed at the Beatles? What did the editor of *America* magazine imply when he said, "Christianity must come alive again in the minds and hearts of the young?"

The songs in this book probe the questions which deeply concern the past, the present, and future of our faith. They are not religious in the traditional sense of the above and beyond, of Sunday Service, of sermons from the pulpit. The songs describe the struggle of growing to be a person in today's world: sharing yourself with others instead of falling into the "Sounds of Silence"; experiencing and bringing to all men the freedom to live in justice and peace in the better world of "Blowin' in the Wind"; loving the special someone of "People"; enjoying the

happiness of the "59th Street Bridge Song"; and, finally, grasping
a reason, an answer to the "why" of each "Day in the Life."
They reveal the evils of a world filled with slums, heroin,
suicides, deserted loves, warring nations, people hiding in their
rooms, and crucifixions; they help us to see it can be changed.
The message is relevant to our lives, phrasing our protest and
our dreams, giving us a "gospel" we can understand and live.
These are "the words of the prophets" spoken to us today.
Growth comes with our personal response to the challenge of
these words.

The teenage years are crucial in the process of growth.
During the evolution from child to man we mature on physical,
emotional, intellectual, and social levels. The parish, the family,
and the school spoon feed us lest we starve and become life-time
losers. Too often, however, parallel spiritual growth is
neglected. We are taught not to "get involved," but to seek
security and success. Our explanation of God matures from a
child's concept of a bearded old man to a legalistic vision of
a Judge upon a throne. The teenager who should see Christ as
brother and friend is often denied new vision at the critical
threshold of his life. The songs in this book should create new
sensitivity to personal relations, awareness of the world and a
new mandate for Christian response. The teenager becomes more
open, growing in his ability to get involved, waking up to the
needs "within him and without him". He begins to see Christ
hungry, thirsty, in need and alive in every person, his friend
and brother.

Hopefully these songs and pictures will be helpful to teacher
and student as well as to pastor and parent. The themes—
communication, freedom, love, happiness, peace—are life's

themes; the questions aim at discovering self-identity, personal fulfillment, and genuine concern for our neighbor. For this is the Christian task.

In addition to discussion in Religion class—Sunday School, CCD, or daily classes—these songs and pictures would be very suitable for group Guidance period. Selections could also be very effective in youth leadership workshops, at religious services, on retreats and days of Christian renewal and similar youth programs. Group discussion on these songs and pictures would be very suitable for teenage ecumenical meetings.

Another important use would be as a bridge to the adult world. These songs could help convey teen attitudes and values to parents and teachers either at parent-teacher meetings or in parent-student discussion groups aimed at nourishing teen-parent understanding.

Though the method of using these songs will vary according to the situation, for the student the first step in his discovery is the experience of listening to the song. For the sounds are part of the message creating an atmosphere that can give new insights to the listener. A second listening while reading the words is often helpful. Next in this process of discovery is sharing your reactions to this experience. This is best accomplished in small groups where talk is free and honest. A typical class can easily be divided in groups of six or seven. It is important that the group foster tolerance and openness in answering the questions. The small group discussion may be given a definite period of time or left open-ended. In either case at some point these groups should summarize their reflections and each group recorder report to the whole group. By so experiencing the songs and pictures with others our experience is enriched.

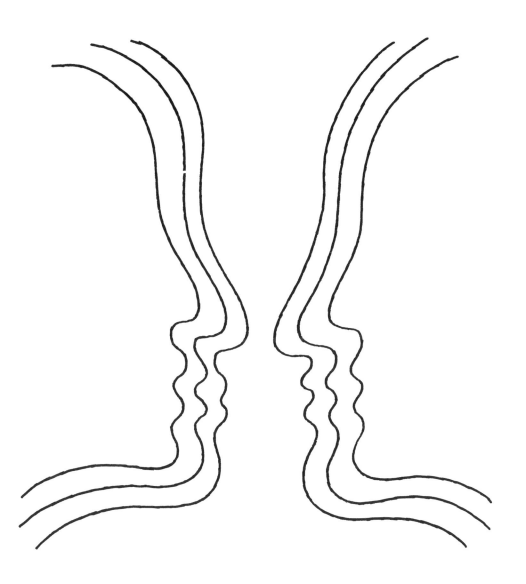

COMMUNICATION

Shells Upon the Shore

"Is it raining outside?" George asks as he sits by his desk in the office. His hellos and goodbyes flood the hours 9 thru 5. There was a time when George would talk about what really mattered to him, but no one seemed to be listening. His words were lost amid financial statements from department #72.

George rides home by train to his split-level outside the city. "Yes, dear, it's been a busy day," he answers Martha. After dinner he lies down on the couch and takes it straight from Huntley and Brinkley. Around ten their daughter Kathy rushes in, slamming the door behind her. "What happened?" they ask. "You wouldn't understand," she mutters, but she sees in their eyes they did not hear her. "Nothing, nothing at all," she sighs as she starts up the stairs.

SHE'S LEAVING HOME *by Lennon and McCartney* (*The Beatles*)

Sometimes you wonder whether your parents are really turned on.

Wednesday morning at five o'clock as the day begins
Silently closing her bedroom door
Leaving the note that she hoped would say more
She goes downstairs to the kitchen clutching her handkerchief
Quietly turning the backdoor key
Stepping outside she is free.

She (we gave her most of our lives)
is leaving (Sacrificed most of our lives)
home (We gave her everything money could buy)
She's leaving home after living alone
For so many years. Bye, bye.

Father snores as his wife gets into her dressing gown
Picks up the letter that's lying there
Standing alone at the top of the stairs
She breaks down and cries to her husband
Daddy our baby's gone.
Why would she treat us so thoughtlessly
How could she do this to me.

She (We never thought of ourselves)
is leaving (Never a thought for ourselves)
home (We struggled hard all our lives to get by)
She's leaving home after living alone
For so many years. Bye, bye.

Friday morning at nine o'clock she is far away
Waiting to keep the appointment she made
Meeting a man from the motor trade.

She (what did we do that was wrong)
is having (We didn't know it was wrong)
fun (Fun is the one thing that money can't buy)
Something inside that was always denied
For so many years. Bye, bye
She's leaving home bye, bye.

"Leaving the note that she hoped would say more . . ." What does this tell us about the girl?

What is revealed about the parents-daughter relationship in the following lines?

"Daddy our baby's gone."

"We gave her everything money could buy."

"She's leaving home after living alone for so many years."

"Why would she treat us so thoughtlessly
How could she do this to me?"
Did the girl really treat her parents "thoughtlessly"? Could she have done otherwise?

What was the "Something inside that was always denied for so many years"? Did she attain this?

What fun does she think "the man from the motor trade" will give her that she didn't receive from her parents?

Why did the parents fail to see that what they did was wrong?

Does leaving home help solve the situation?

Describe a typical "Nowhere Man."

Is the "Nowhere Man making all his plans for nobody" the same as the parents "sacrificing most of our lives" (from "She's Leaving Home")?

Compare: "He's as blind as he can be,
Just sees what he wants to see."
with the parents' lines of "She's Leaving Home":
"What did we do that was wrong?
we didn't know it was wrong."

Compare: "Something inside that was always denied"
(from "She's Leaving Home")
with "Nowhere man, please listen.
You don't know what you're missin'."

18

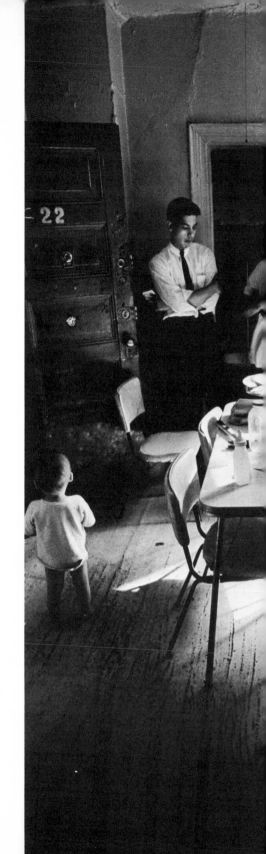

NOWHERE MAN *by Lennon and McCartney* *(Beatles)*

Sometimes it's better not to have an opinion, 'cause then you can't be wrong. Sometimes it's better not to get involved with people 'cause then there're no tears. Sometimes it's better not to live.

Nowhere man 7:11-13.

He's a real nowhere man,
Sitting in his nowhere land,
Making all his nowhere plans for nobody.

Doesn't have a point of view,
Knows not where he's going to.
Isn't he a bit like you and me?

Nowhere man, please listen.
You don't know what you're missin'.
Nowhere man, the world is at your command.

He's as blind as he can be,
Just sees what he wants to see.
Nowhere man, can you see me at all?

Nowhere man, don't worry.
Take your time; don't hurry.
Leave it all till somebody else lends you a hand.

Doesn't have a point of view,
Knows not where he's going to.
Isn't he a bit like you and me?

Nowhere man, please listen.
You don't know what you're missin'.
Nowhere man, the world is at your command.

He's a real nowhere man,
Sitting in his nowhere land,
Making all his nowhere plans for nobody.

Simon and Garfunkel's "Sounds of Silence" is, in the words of Art Garfunkel, "a major work." "Its theme," writes Garfunkel, "is man's inability to communicate with man . . . The words tell us that when meaningful communication fails, the only sound is silence." But there is a positive aspect to the Sounds of Silence, as revealed in the lines:

"'The words of the prophets are written
on the subway walls,
And tenement halls,
And whisper in the sounds of silence.'"

What is the significance of "darkness"? Why is it "my old friend"?

What is the point of the "vision" spoken of in the third line?

Why does Garfunkel say that the neon sign is representative of the "most superficial and 'commercial' level of communication"?

What is the point of the lines:
"People talking without speaking,
People hearing without listening,
People writing songs that voices
never share . . ."

In the fourth verse the speaker tries to destroy the sounds of silence. Is he successful?

". . . He planted a cedar and the rain made it grow. For the common man it is so much fuel; he uses it to warm himself, he also burns it to bake his bread. But this fellow makes a god of it and worships it; he makes an idol of it and bows down before it . . . with the rest he makes his god, his idol; he bows down before it and worships it and prays to it. 'Save me,' he says, 'because you are my god.' They know nothing, understand nothing. Their eyes are shut to all seeing, their heart to all reason. They never think . . ."
—ISAIAH 44:14–19.
Compare this quote to the first two lines of the last verse.

What is the message of the "sign" at the end of the song? What is the relationship to the rest of the song?

THE SOUNDS OF SILENCE *by P. Simon (Simon and Garfunkel)*

Hello, darkness, my old friend,
I've come to talk with you again.
Because a vision softly creeping
Left its seeds while I was sleeping,
And the vision that was planted in my brain
Still remains,
Within the sound of silence.

In restless dreams I walked alone
Through narrow streets of cobblestone,
'Neath the halo of a street lamp,
I turned my collar to the cold and damp,
When my eyes were stabbed by the flash of a neon light.
It split the night.
And touched the sound of silence.

And in the naked light I saw
Ten thousand people, maybe more,
People talking without speaking,
People hearing without listening,
People writing songs that voices never share . . .
No one dared
Disturb the sound of silence.

"Fools," said I, "you do not know,
Silence like a cancer grows;
Hear my words that I might teach you.
Take my arms that I might reach you."
But my words, like silent rain-drops, fell,
And echoed in the wells of silence.

And the people bowed and prayed
To the neon god they made,
And the sign burst out its warning,
In the words that it was forming,
And the sign said: "The words of the prophets are written
on the subway walls,
And tenement halls,
And whisper in the sounds of silence."

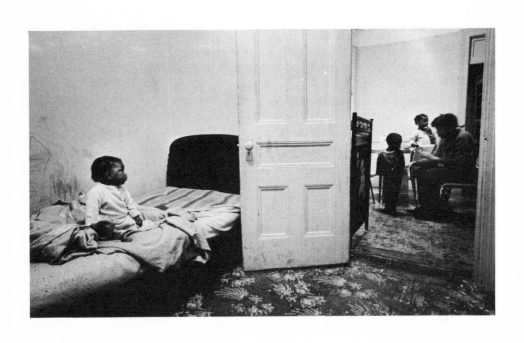

LITTLE BOXES *words & music by Malvina Reynolds (Pete Seeger)*

Little Boxes

Little boxes, on the hillside,
Little boxes, made of ticky-tacky,
Little boxes, little boxes, little boxes, all the same.
There's a green one and a pink one and a
blue one and a yellow one,
And they're all made out of ticky-tacky and
they all look just the same.

And the people in the houses all go to the University,
Where they all get put in boxes, little boxes, all the same,
And there's doctors and there's lawyers and business executives,
And they're all made out of ticky-tacky and they all look just the
 same.

And they all play on the golf-course and drink their martinis dry,
And they all have pretty children and the children go to school.
And the children go to summer camp and then to the University,
And they all get put in boxes and they all come out the same.

And the boys go into business and marry and raise a family,
And they all get put in boxes, little boxes, all the same.
There's a green one, and a pink one, and a blue one, and a yellow
 one,
And they're all made out of ticky-tacky and they all look just the
 same.

PENNY LANE *Lennon and McCartney* (*The Beatles*)

The Beatles' "Penny Lane," like most rock and roll hits, is rarely studied in depth. Although very subtle, it has a message similar to that of "Little Boxes." In our suburbanized society communication breaks down to pleasantries.

Penny Lane

On Penny Lane there is a barber showing photographs
Of every head he's had the pleasure to know,
And all the people that come and go
Stop and say hello.

On the corner is a banker with a motor car.
The little children laugh at him behind his back,
And the banker never wears a mac,
In the pouring rain . . .
Very strange.

Refrain:
Penny Lane is in my ears and in my eyes,
Wet beneath the blue suburban skies
I sit and meanwhile back . . .

In Penny Lane there is a fireman with an hourglass,
And in his pocket is a portrait of the queen,
He likes to keep his fire engine clean.
It's a clean machine.

Penny Lane is in my ears and in my eyes,
Full of fish and finger pies in summer . . .
Meanwhile back . . .

Behind the shelter in the middle of the roundabout,
A pretty nurse is selling poppies from a tray,
And though she feels as if she's in a play,
She is anyway.

Penny Lane: the barber shaves another customer,
We see the banker sitting waiting for a trend
And then the fireman rushes in,
From the pouring rain . . .
Very strange . . .

What are the different "boxes" that are mentioned in the first song?

What is the connection between the line "And there's doctors and there's lawyers and business executives" and the characters in "Penny Lane"?

How does the idea of a "box" relate to the imagery of "shells upon the shore" and "borders" in "The Dangling Conversation"?

Is there similarity between the activities of the people inside the "little boxes" and the line in "Penny Lane" "and though she feels as if she's in a play, she is anyway"?

What word in the refrain of "Penny Lane" is reminiscent of the scene in "Little Boxes"?

The artist in "Penny Lane" says something is "very strange." What is?

The "clean machine" is Penny Lane. Compare it with these lines from "Little Boxes":
"And they all get put in boxes, little boxes, all the same,
There's a green one, and a pink one, and a blue one, and a
    yellow one,
And they're all made out of ticky-tacky and they all look just the
    same."

Does the writer of "Little Boxes" add to her message by the sounds of the words she repeats?

I THINK IT'S GOING TO RAIN TODAY *by Newman* (*Judy Collins*)

"I Think It's Going to Rain Today," sung by Judy Collins, is a bitter attack on life as we know it. Using sarcasm to a peak of effectiveness, she stresses the great contrasts within our own society. After speaking about loneliness and the manner in which friends treat each other, the singer reminds us of the duties we have toward the poor. The very real connection to communication contained in this song becomes evident to the listener with a little thought.

Broken windows and empty hallways
A pale dead moon in a sky streaked with gray
Human kindness is overflowing and I
Think it's going to rain today

Scarecrows dressed in the latest styles with
Frozen smiles to chase love away
Human kindness is overflowing and I
Think it's going to rain today

Lonely————————
Lonely————————
Tin can at my feet think I'll kick
It down the street
That's the way to treat a friend

Bright before me the signs implore me
"Help the needy and show them the way"
Human kindness why it's overflowing and I
Think it's going to rain today

What is the overall effect of the images used in the first two lines? Is this related to communication?

Do you think the line, "Human kindness overflowing," is sarcastic?

Who are the "scarecrows dressed in the latest styles"?

Who is "lonely . . . lonely" and why?

The fourth verse (Marked #3) seems to be a call for positive action. Relate this verse to the preceding ones.

Compare the following common statements. Notice one is the key line. Discover its function in the song.
"I think it's going to rain today"
"Hot enough for you?"
"This weather is something, isn't it?"

Is there a connection between the lines:
"I think it's going to rain today" and
"Help the needy and show them the way"?

Does the sound of "lonely . . . lonely" add to the meaning?

DANGLING CONVERSATION
by P. Simon (Simon and Garfunkel)

"Dangling Conversation" paints a picture of a relationship that has degenerated until it is almost without meaning. The two characters of the song no longer say what they want to communicate. Instead they ask impersonal questions like: Is the theater dead? Is analysis really worthwhile?

The first verse presents a picture. What does the late afternoon indicate about the stage of the relationship between the two people?

What is the connection between the title and the imagery of the song, e.g. verses without rhythm and rhyme, etc?

The two persons have become indifferent. How does this fit in with the image of shells on the seashore? Why is the fact that one hears the ocean roaring brought up?

How does the border of our life relate to the imagery of the shells on the seashore?

Contrast the line stating that you are a stranger to me with the afternoon scene at the beginning of the song. How does this reveal the change in the relationship between the two people?

How does the sound of the music and the mood it creates fit in with the meaning of the lyrics, e.g. the ocean roaring?

THE FLOWER LADY *by Phil Ochs (Jim and Jean, "Pleasures of the Harbor" A&M LP4133)*

"Flower Lady" by Phil Ochs paints a scene from the heart of the city. The poet describes the panorama of our society-millionaires, paupers, lovers, and poets, soldiers and students, and the aged— all centered around a woman selling flowers. Their words and efforts to communicate are subtly compared to the simple message in a flower.

Millionaires and paupers walk the hungry streets
Rich and poor companions of a restless dream
Strangers in a foreign land
Strike a match with a trembling hand
They're too much to ever understand
But nobody's buying flowers from the flower lady.

Lovers quarrel, snarl away their happiness.
Kisses crumble in a web of loneliness.
It's written by the poison pen.
Voices break before they bend.
The door is slammed. It's over once again
But nobody's buying flowers from the flower lady.

Poets agonize—they cannot find the words
The stone stares at the sculptor (has stunned you absurd)
The painter paints his brushes black.
Through the canvas runs a crack
Portrait of the pain never answers back
But nobody's buying flowers from the flower lady.

Soldiers disillusioned come home from the war
Sarcastic students tell them not to fight no more
And they argue through the night
Black is black and white is white
Walk away both knowing they are right
But nobody's buying flowers from the flower lady.

People, aged people, almost to their knees
Complain about the present using memories
Never found their pot of gold
(wrinkled hands found weary hold)
Each line screams out: You're old, you're old, you're old
But nobody's buying flowers from the flower lady.

And the flower lady hobbles home without a sale
Tattered shreds of petals leave a fading trail
Not a cause to call her own
Even she no longer knows
The lamp goes out—the evening is closed.
But nobody's buying flowers from the flower lady.

Why are people described as "strangers in a foreign land"?

"Voices break before they bend.
The door is slammed. It's over once again"
Does this recall some typical human experience?

Artists are described in the third stanza. What is the common result of their efforts?

"And they argue through the night
Black is black and white is white
Walk away both knowing they are right."
How do you remedy such a situation?

The Flower Lady stands as the unifying element in the song. Why is she overlooked by all the other people?

PEOPLE *by Styne-Merrill* (*Barbra Streisand*)

Barbra Streisand's "People" is, like "Alfie" and "Georgy Girl," an attempt to get down to "what it's all about." The first step towards love, the singer tells us, is to "be a person who needs people."

People who recognize their need of other people do not allow their false pride to restrain their actions. Once someone is in love, he feels personally fulfilled; yet, this cannot happen unless he first is open to others.

What does the phrase "letting our grownup pride hide all the need inside" say about person to person communication?

What do you think is meant by the words, "Acting more like children than children"?

Why are lovers "very special people"?

Why does ". . . a feeling deep in your soul say you were half, now you're whole"?

Is the good fortune of lovers what is missing in Simon and Garfunkel's "Dangling Conversation"?

What is the stress of the lines:
". . . No more hunger and thirst.
But first, be a person who needs people"?

WHAT A GREAT THING IT IS *by Ray Repp* (*Ray Repp*)

Refrain: What a great thing it is
           (What a great thing it is)
And oh how pleasant it can be
           (Oh how pleasant it can be)
For all God's people to live together in peace.
So now tell everyone you meet
           (Now tell everyone you meet)
The joy that we were meant to see
           (Joy that we were meant to see)
           (When all God's people live together in peace.)

The Lord gave everyone the law that we should
love and follow every call from Him.
LOVE AND FOLLOW EVERY CALL FROM HIM.

Refrain.

The Father promised us a home where we could
live together as a family.
LIVE TOGETHER AS A FAMILY.

Refrain.

Brothers, sisters, are we all because we're
made as equal in the sight of God.
MADE AS EQUAL IN THE SIGHT OF GOD.

Refrain.

All you children of the Lord sing out and
praise our God for all eternity
PRAISE OUR GOD FOR ALL ETERNITY.

Refrain.

How can we communicate "The joy
that we were meant to see/When all
God's people live together in peace"?
"We're made as equal in the sight of
God."
What is this equality? How should
this foster our communication with
others as brothers and sisters? Is this
connected with the communication
that existed in "She's Leaving Home"?
"WE could live together as a family/
Live together as a family."
How does communication fit into this
picture?

Appendix

1 *Pleasant Valley Sunday (The Monkees)—the American "Penny Lane"*

2 *Sooner or Later One of Us Must Know (Bob Dylan)—the bitter taste of love grown cold*

3 *Downtown (Petula Clark)—instant route to happiness*

4 *Most Peculiar Man (Simon and Garfunkel)—"he lived . . . within himself"*

5 *What Did You Learn in School Today? (Pete Seeger)—do we get the truth in school?*

FREEDOM

Tear Down the Walls

Through the heat of the city a teenager walks, a button on his shirt proclaiming, "I know what's happening, Mr. Jones." He overhears a sidewalk Socrates philosophizing on how rotten kids are these days. He listens as the well-tailored businessmen talk stock averages in the neat canyons of skyscrapers. He times the heads turning as a mixed couple stroll by, hand in hand. A few blocks later he sees beneath a tenement a copy of ELIJAH SPEAKS in the gutter.

On the radio at home he sometimes hears the rebellious voice of youth, the outcry of the oppressed, the fear that we are only cogs in a machine, children of society, puppets of fate. Soon he turns off the music, knowing his parents will think it too loud, knowing Harlem means as much to him as last year's textbooks, knowing that no matter what we do the wheels keep turning.

PATTERNS *by P. Simon* (*Simon and Garfunkel*)

Paul Simon describing "Patterns" said that he was on an existential kick for a while, and he wrote a song called "Patterns," concerned with the fact that our lives are broken down into so many patterns that we have no control over—the color of our skins, the fact that we die. We have no control over these patterns. We can't change them. They affect your whole life; where you were born, what your name is.

What is the importance of the nighttime setting and the isolation of the hero?

Do you see any significance in the imagery of the uneven scrawl of a child or pieces of the puzzle?

What is the function of a pattern in society? in our society?

How does the word "narrow" affect the mood and meaning of the patterns?

What happens if the person does not follow the patterns? In the scheme of the song, is there any place for personal freedom?

Trace the various musical patterns and how they complement the words.

I WANNA BE FREE *Words & Music by Tommy Boyce & Bobby Hart (The Monkees)*

In high school things begin to bug you. You notice how your parents police you. Everybody has rules. You want to get away and just be yourself.

I wanna be free, like the bluebirds flying by me
Like the waves along the blue sea.
If your love has to tie me, don't try me who-o-o-oa

I wanna be free, don't say you love me, say you like me
But when I need you beside me
Stay close enough to guide me, confide in me, who-o-o-oa

I want to hold your hand, walk along the sand,
Laughing in the sun, always having fun
Doing all those things without any strings to tie me down.

I wanna be free, like the warm September winds, babe
Say you'll always be my friend, babe,
We can make it to the end, babe, again, babe, who-o-o-oa.
I wanna be free, I wanna be free, I wanna be free.

Why like, not love?

How does the writer feel love restricts freedom?

What is the concept of freedom in the song?

"We can make it to the end." What "end" are they talking about?

How does the line "Hearts, they shrink, pockets swell," contrast with the preceding two lines?

Do you think Caesar or Caesar's men are worthy of more criticism in the singer's eyes?

What role do the "pious citizens" play?

Why "blame the angels," "fates," "Jews," "or your sister Kate"?

Buffy Sainte-Marie says: "Teach your children who to hate." Bob Dylan sings in "Only a Pawn in their Game":

But the poor white man's used in the
    hands of them all like a tool.
He's taught in his school from the
    start by the rule
That the laws are with him to protect
    his white skin
To keep up his hate so he never
    thinks straight
'bout the shape that he's in
But it ain't him to blame,
He's only a pawn in their game.

Is there any difference? Discuss.

How do little wheels "teach your children who to hate"?

What is the irony of "Pray like hell when the world explodes"?

LITTLE WHEEL SPIN AND SPIN *by Buffy Sainte-Marie* (*Buffy Sainte-Marie*)

Buffy Sainte-Marie's "Little Wheel Spin and Spin" is a powerful protest against the state of the "little wheel," or the little man. While the "little" people are subtly conditioned to continue the established order, the song tells us, "the big wheel turns round and round." While the little wheels "teach (their) children who to hate, the evils in the system are perpetuated.

Little wheel spin and spin, big wheel turn round and round (4x)

Merry Christmas, jingle bells,
Christ is born and the devil's in hell
Hearts, they shrink, pockets swell
Everybody know and nobody tell.

Little wheel spin and spin, big wheel turn round and round (2x)

Oh, the sins of Caesar's men
Cried the pious citizens
Petty thieves of the five and ten
And the big wheel turn round and round.

Little wheel spin and spin, big wheel turn round and round (2x)

Blame the angels, blame the fates,
Blame the Jews, or your sister Kate,
Teach your children who to hate,
And the big wheel turn round and round.

Little wheel spin and spin, big wheel turn round and round (2x)

Turn your back on weeds you've hoed
Silly sinful seeds you've sowed
Add your straw to the camel's load
Pray like hell when the world explodes.

Little wheel spin and spin, big wheel turn round and round (2x)

Swing your girl, fiddler say,
Later on the piper played.
Do-see-doe, swing and sway
Devil dance on judgment day

Little wheel spin and spin, big wheel turn round and round (4x)

Used by permission © Gypsy Boy Music, Inc., 1966.

Does the song equate loss of ability to "be astounded" with loss of freedom?

Can the dimensions of freedom spelled out in the song be summed up in "Let's not complicate our minds"?

Do you see any difference between the phrases "walls to divide you" and "no need to hide" in relation to freedom?

To what extent are all men "born free"?

"Born free, as free as the wind blows." Does the music match this description of freedom?

BORN FREE *Music by John Barry, Lyric by Don Black*
(*R. Williams*)

Have you ever been out on an October day looking at a sunset, watching the birds fly south? Have you ever wished that you could go with them?

Born free, as free as the wind blows,
As free as the grass grows,
Born free to follow your heart.

Live free, and beauty surrounds you
The world still astounds you each time you look at a star.

Stay free, where no walls divide you,
You're free as a roaring tide so there's no need to hide.

Born free, and life is worth living,
But only worth living 'cause you're born free.

LINKS ON THE CHAIN *by Phil Ochs* (*Phil Ochs*)

Racial equality has been strong in policy but weak in practice of American unionism. Phil Ochs sees this as a betrayal of unionism's bloody birth.

Come you ranks of labor, come you union core,
And see if you remember the struggles of before,
When you were standing helpless on the outside of the door,
And you started building links on the chain, on the chain,
And you started building links on the chain.

When the police on the horses were waitin' on demand,
Ridin' through the strike with the pistols in their hands,
Swingin' at the skulls of many a union man,
As you built one more link on the chain, on the chain,
As you built one more link on the chain.

Then the army of the fascists tried to put you on the run,
But the army of the union, they did what could be done,
Oh, the power of the factory was greater than the gun,
As you built one more link on the chain, on the chain,
As you built one more link on the chain.

And then in 1954, decisions finally made,
The black man was a-risin' fast and racin' from the shade,
And your union took no stand and your union was betrayed,
As you lost yourself a link on the chain, on the chain,
As you lost yourself a link on the chain.

And then there came the boycotts and then the freedom rides,
And forgetting what you stood for, you tried to block the tide,
Oh, the automation bosses were laughin' on the side,
As they watched you lose your link on the chain, on the chain,
As they watched you lose your link on the chain.

You know when they block your trucks boys, by layin' on the
                road,
All that they are doin' is all that you have showed,
That you gotta strike, you gotta fight to get what you are owed,
When you're building all your links on the chain, on the chain,
When you're building all your links on the chain.

And the man who tries to tell you that they'll take your job away,
He's the same man who was scabbin' hard just the other day,
And your union's not a union till he's thrown out of the way,
And he's chokin' on your links of the chain, of the chain,
And he's chokin' on your links of the chain.

For now the times are tellin' you the times are rollin' on,
And you're fighting for the same thing, the jobs that will be gone,
Now it's only fair to ask you boys, which side are you on
As you're buildin' all your links on the chain, on the chain,
As you're buildin' all your links on the chain.

At whose demand were the police breaking strikes in early union days?

Did the "boycotts" and "freedom rides" of the early '60's nourish or hamper our freedom?

Is it true "That you gotta strike, you gotta fight to get what you are owed"?

What are the "links on the chain"?

How does an individual person's building "the links on the chain" in his personal life differ from a union or group's building "links on the chain"?

Do you agree that the man "who tries to tell you that they'll take your job away" is chokin' the links on the chain?

A Research Question:
A. What was the attitude of the main labor unions toward integration in 1954?

B. What is their attitude toward integration today?

C. Does their practice differ or agree with their public attitude?

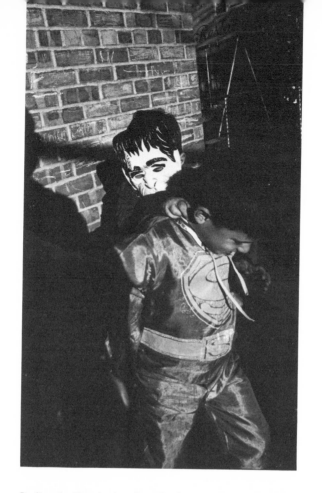

What is the significance of the changes in the two words preceding each refrain?

What attitude does the line "But for now this is the way they must remain" reveal? Do you feel this attitude is justified or mature?

How do the teachers "cut deep down" in their affairs?

Why is she "society's child"?

"One of these days I'm gonna stop my listenin'." Are these words familiar to you?

What does the shrill organ music at the end of the song suggest to you?

What do you think of parents who allow their sons and daughters to date with young people of another race?

SOCIETY'S CHILD by *Janis Ian* (*Janis Ian*)

"Society's Child" is one of the most controversial songs of our time. Dealing with the subject of inter-racial dating, the song was at first banned by many overcautious disc jockeys. Here is one practical area where one can ask whether the Gospel is merely a collection of empty words irrelevant to our personal lives.

Come to my door, baby
Face is clean and shining black as night
My mother went to answer, you know that you looked so fine
Now I could understand your tears and your shame
She called you boy instead of your name.
When she wouldn't let you inside
When she turned and said but honey he's not our kind.

She says: I can't see you any more, baby
　　　can't see you any more

Walk me down to school, baby
Everybody's actin' deaf and dumb
Until they turn and say, "why don't you stick to your own kind?"
My teachers all laugh, the smirking stares,
Cuttin' deep down in our affairs
Preachers of equality, think they believe it;
Then why won't they just let us be?

They say: I can't see you any more, baby
　　　can't see you any more.

One of these days I'm going to stop my listenin'
Gonna raise my head up high
One of these days I'm gonna raise up my glistenin' wings and fly.
But that day will have to wait for a while.
Baby, I'm only society's child.
When we're older things may change
But for now this is the way they must remain.

I say: I can't see you any more, baby
　　　can't see you any more.
No, I don't wanna see you any more, baby.

Do you feel any personal concern for the American Indian? Do you feel you are responsible for the misdeeds of your countrymen both in the present and past?

How would you feel about the government if you were an Indian? What would you do? Would violence be justified?

Do the Indians have any rights to lands just because they once owned them? Do you feel the Indians should control those lands which they still own legally by treaty?

The United States Supreme Court may soon decide in favor of the Indian claim to a large part of the State of Florida. How would you react if this was decided in favor of the Indians?

Would Christ have killed an Indian for the sake of progress?

NOW THAT THE BUFFALOES' GONE *by Buffy Sainte-Marie*
(*Buffy Sainte-Marie*)

What we know about the Indians usually comes from the movies and TV, where the civilized white man invariably triumphs over the red savage. We are not familiar with a history of treaties made and broken by our government, of the smallpox that accompanied the dead soldiers' blankets the agent distributed on the reservation, of the millions of dead buffaloes, of a way of life and people sacrificed to progress. But the dead cry out for retribution.

Can you remember the time that you have held your head high
And told all your friends of your Indian claim,
Proud good lady and proud good man;
Your great-great grandfather from Indian blood sprang,
And you feel in your hearts for these ones.

Oh, it's written in books and in songs,
That we've been mistreated and wronged;
Well over and over I hear the same words,
From you good lady and you good man,
Well listen to me if you care where we stand
And you feel you're a part of these ones.

When a war between nations is lost,
The loser we know pays the cost;
But even when Germany fell to your hands,
Consider, dear lady, consider, dear man,
You left them their pride and you left them their lands,
And what have you done for these ones?

Has a change come about Uncle Sam,
Or are you still taking our lands?
A treaty forever George Washington signed;
He did, dear lady, he did, dear man.
And the treaty's being broken by Kinsula Dam,
And what will you do for these ones?

Oh, it's all in the past, you may say,
But it's still going on here today:
The government now wants the Iroquois lands,
That of the Seneca and the Cheyenne.
It's here and it's now you must help us dear man,
Now that the buffaloes' gone.

THE LONESOME DEATH OF HATTIE CARROLL *by Bob Dylan* (*Bob Dylan*)

This tragic ballad by Bob Dylan is an allegory on the history of the race problem in our country. The white man and the black man are symbolized in William Zanzinger and his victim, Hattie Carroll. The song reminds us that "the land of the free" is often a hollow platitude.

Who is more free: William Zanzinger or Hattie Carroll?

Stanzas two and three present biographical sketches of William Zanzinger and Hattie Carroll. What do their economic conditions tell us about freedom in America?

Why is Hattie Carroll's death lonesome?

Who is the "you" in the refrain?

Why, after William Zanzinger is jailed for six months, is it time for tears?

Do you think that the history of Hattie Carroll is related to the recent riots?

POWER AND GLORY *by Phil Ochs* (*Phil Ochs*)

Patriotism has become a dirty word in recent years. Flag burnings, draft resistance, blood sent to the Viet Cong, and imprecations against the President are more commonplace than The Star Spangled Banner. *In the midst of this corrosion of our national character, Phil Ochs defines what it is to be an American in* Power and Glory.

C'mon and take a walk with me through this green and growin'
        land,
Walk through the meadows and the mountains and the sand,
Walk through the valleys and the rivers and the plains,
Walk through the sun and walk through the rain.

Refrain
Here's a land full of power and glory
Beauty that words cannot recall
Oh her power shall rest on the strength of her freedom
Her glory shall rest on us all. (2. From all, on us all.)

From Colorado, Kansas and the Carolinas, too,
Virginia and Alaska, from the old to the new,
Texas and Ohio and the California shore,
Tell me who could ask for more.

Refrain

Yet she's only as rich as the poorest of the poor,
Only as free as a padlocked prison door,
Only as strong as our love for this land,
Only as tall as we stand.

Refrain

Repeat Verse One

Refrain

Phil Ochs regularly attends peace rallies and protests against the Vietnamese war. He himself says this song is about "real patriotism, not just something to wave a flag about." Is he being consistent?

"She's only as rich as the poorest of the poor
Only as free as a padlocked prison door."
The writer is criticizing certain evils in our society. Is this patriotic?

Does the glory of this land rest on us all? Is the democratic spirit of this song outdated?

To what does a citizen owe his loyalty—the ideals of a nation or its governmental structure? What happens if the two conflict?

Would you like to see this song or Woody Guthrie's This Land Is Your Land become our national anthem?

Do you feel that you can significantly affect decision making process in this country?

Hans J. Morgenthau of the University of Chicago writes in the October 28, 1967 edition of THE NEW REPUBLIC: "The great national decisions of life and death are rendered by technological elites, and both the Congress and the people at large retain little more than the illusion of making the decisions which the theory of democracy supposes them to make." Do you agree?

To whom is the message of the song addressed?

Why are the sons and daughters really beyond their parents' command?

Your old way is rapidly failing; if you do not lend a hand please leave the new one. What are mothers and fathers obstructing?

What is the struggle the senators and congressmen are hindering?

What kind of freedom is implied in stanza three (stanza concerning senators and congressmen)? In stanza four (concerning mothers and fathers)?

The first one will later become last. Does this resemble any of Christ's teaching?

Jesus said: "If you dwell within the revelation I have brought, you are indeed my disciples; you shall know the truth, and the truth will set you free." (Jn. 8.32)

Is living the truth of these songs the same as living the truth of revelation?

THE TIMES THEY ARE A-CHANGIN' by Bob Dylan (Bob Dylan)

Bob Dylan lyricized the freedom revolution in our country in "The Times They Are A-Changin'." A rousing song, almost a battle cry, it speaks of freedom on both the personal and social levels. Like many other protest songs, its message also contains a warning that is blood-chilling in its truthfulness.

Appendix

1 Birmingham Sunday (Joan Baez)—four girls killed in a church by "Christians"

2 Big Bright Green Pleasure Machine (Simon and Garfunkel)—Madison Avenue: "we can neutralize your brain"

3 Oh Freedom (Pete Seeger)—"give me liberty or give me death"

4 There but for Fortune (Phil Ochs)—Fate in human life

5 It Isn't Nice (Judy Collins)—the struggle for justice sometimes hurts

6 He Was My Brother (Simon and Garfunkel)—Brotherhood, U.S.A.

7 This Land Is Your Land (Woody Guthrie)—a beautiful nation that belongs to us all

8 Tear Down the Walls (Judy Collins)—freedom and brotherhood go hand-in-hand

LOVE

Oaks and Willows

St. Paul tells us that we must love. Mick Jagger tells us to love. Love overflows everywhere. Free love. Love for sale. Love on a rooftop. Love makes the world go 'round. Love is a many splendored thing. You can't hurry love. Love God. Love your neighbor. Love is alive and well in Duluth, Minnesota. And so human beings love, procreate their kind, and pass away. Love, promised cure-all for the world, still leaves us Vietnams and Harlems; it still leaves us husbands and wives bickering through the night and crowded divorce courts; it still leaves tears on the face of a young girl at her window and a boy wondering if the years can heal the wound in his heart.

ELEANOR RIGBY *by Lennon and McCartney* (*Beatles*)

The lonely people peep through the curtainlace, opening their doors for a brief look at the outside world, then quickly retreat into the weblike microcosm of self. They can make it all alone.

Ah, look at all the lonely people
Ah, look at all the lonely people,

Eleanor Rigby picks up the rice in the church where a wedding
has been
Lives in a dream.
Waits at the window wearing a face that she keeps in a jar by
the door
Who is it for?

All the lonely people: where do they all come from?
All the lonely people: where do they all belong?

Father McKenzie writing the words of a sermon that no one will
hear
No one comes near
Look at him working: darning his socks in the night when there's
nobody there
What does he care?

All the lonely people: where do they all come from?
All the lonely people: where do they all belong?

Ah, look at all the lonely people
Ah, look at all the lonely people.

Eleanor Rigby died in the church and was buried along with her
name
Nobody came.
Father McKenzie wiping the dirt from his hands as he walks
from the grave
No one was saved.

All the lonely people: where do they all come from?
        Ah, look at all the lonely people.
All the lonely people: where do they all belong?
        Ah, look at all the lonely people.

Who are the lonely people? Just Eleanor Rigby and Father McKenzie?

Why doesn't Eleanor Rigby come out of her dream? Father McKenzie wipes dirt from his hands as he walks from the grave. Why?

Both Eleanor Rigby and Father McKenzie are connected with the church. Do the Beatles imply anything by this association? How can people so saintly be so lonely?

Do Eleanor Rigby and Father McKenzie ever feel their loneliness? Are they conscious of it?

"No man is an island," writes John Donne in his XVII Meditation, "entire of itself; every man is a piece of the continent, a part of the main. . . . any man's death diminishes me, because I am involved in mankind; and therefore never send to know for whom the bell tolls, it tolls for thee." Do you feel this when the funeral bell tolls for Eleanor Rigby?

What kind of society produces Eleanor Rigbys? Where do they come from?

How does your past age of "wondrous things to be seen and be done" have an effect on your teen years and your attitudes?

"Going steady was all the rage." Do you see any value in going steady at thirteen?

"Mama picked me out the cutest boy." Would your mother pick you out the cutest boy or the richest boy? Do you think your parents can pick out anyone for you?

Does marriage at sixteen years of age have any more promise than at twenty or more? Would you want to marry at sixteen?

When do young adults work on "getting noticed" by the boys (or girls)? Does it seem like they're all playing a game? Do you find yourself playing the game?

Would you agree that life is almost over at twenty-one? What has she lived for? Is there nothing else in life but the ritual of reproduction?

HAIR OF SPUN GOLD *by Janis Ian* (*Janis Ian*)

There is nothing so wasted as youth burnt out at twenty-one.

When I was just the age of five
My world had just come alive;
Wondrous things to be seen and done;
All that I could think of was fun.
With hair of spun gold,
Lips of ruby red
And eyes as deep as the deepest sea.

And when I was just the age of ten
My life, it did change again.
I threw away all my childish toys
And worked on getting noticed by the boys

When I was thirteen years of age
Going steady was all the rage.
Mama picked me out the cutest boy,
My little leather jacketed toy.
And hair of spun gold,
Turned to black as the night;
Lips of ruby red turned to pale pink.

When I was sixteen years of age
He held my hand in marriage
And when sixteen years of age,
In my arms I held my babe.

Now I'm twenty-one, you know;
Feel my life is over and done
And I'm looking down on my child,
Wondering if she'll be so wild.
She's got hair of spun gold,
Lips of ruby red
And eyes as deep as the deepest sea.

And I'm looking down on my child
I swear she'll have the time
There'll be time to love—there'll be time to learn—
for childish memories she won't yearn.
Time to laugh and find time to play;
She won't have to throw her toys away.
I swear to you we'll wait for time to take its time.

WITHIN YOU, WITHOUT YOU *by George Harrison* (*Beatles*)

"Within You, Without You," put to the music of mystical sitar, probes the essential oneness of us all. Beneath the masks of nationality and race men are brothers, sharing a common conscience and life. The conflict between selfishness and the selflessness of our true self becomes the greatest struggle in love.

We were talking—about the space between us all
And the people—who hide themselves
behind a wall of illusion
Never glimpse the truth—then it's far too late—
when they pass away.

We were talking—about the love we all
could share—when we find it
To try our best to hold it there—with our love
With our love—we could save the world
—if they only knew.
Try to realize it's all within yourself
no-one else can make you change
And to see you're really only very small,
and life flows on within you and without you.

We were talking—about the love that's
gone so cold and the people,
who gain the world and lose their soul—
they don't know—they can't see—are you one of them?
When you've seen beyond yourself—
then you may find, peace of mind, is waiting there—
And the time will come when you see
We're all one, and life flows on within you and without you.

What is the "wall of illusion" that
people hide behind?

"Try to realize it's all within yourself
no-one else can make you change"
Is it true that the change can only
come from within?

Explain: "life flows on within you
and without you."

"Are you one of them?"

"When you've seen beyond yourself—
then you may find, peace of mind,
is waiting there—"

How are love and peace of mind
related?

What do they mean by "when you see
we're all one"?

ALFIE *by B. Bacharach and H. David* (*Dionne Warwick*)

The song "Alfie" is taken from the popular movie about a play-boy in urban society. Its significance is universal, however, for it asks questions that are relevant to all our lives.

What's it all about, Alfie,
Is it just for the moment we live?
What's it all about,
When you sort it out, Alfie,
Are we meant to take more than we give,
Or are we meant to be kind?

And if only fools are kind, Alfie,
Then I guess it is wise to be cruel,
And if life belongs
Only to the strong,
What will you mend on an old, golden rule?

As sure as I believe
There's a Heaven above, Alfie,
I know there's something much more,
Something even non-believers
Can believe in:

I believe in love, Alfie,
Without true love, we just exist, Alfie,
Until you find love
You've missed, you're nothing, Alfie . . .

When you walk let your heart lead the way,
And you'll find love any day, Alfie.

What is suggested by the line "is it just for the moment we live"?

Those who love are charac-terized as "fools" by Alfie, but Alfie is himself pictured as "nothing" by the singer. Explain the bases of their viewpoints.

What is the meaning of the phrase "without true love, we just exist—"?

" . . . let your heart lead the way, And you'll find love any day, Alfie."
Do you think this is a realistic attitude?

How does the "hippy" idea of be-ing and Love compare with Alfie's existence?

Is there any clash between the melody and the questions in the song?

I'M A BELIEVER *by Neil Diamond (The Monkees)*

"The first cut is always the deepest" says Sandy Posey. The Monkees seem to have found a cure.

I thought love was only true in fairy tales.
Meant for someone else but not for me.
Love was out to get me.
That's the way it seemed,
Disappointment haunted all my dreams.

Refrain:
Then I saw her face, now I'm a believer!
Not a trace of doubt in my mind.
I'm in love, I'm a believer.
I couldn't leave her if I tried.

I thought love was more or less a given thing.
Seems more I gave, the less I got.
What's the use of tryin'?
All you get is pain.
When I needed sunshine I got rain.

Refrain:

What is the difference in attitude
between the verses and the
refrain?

What does he "believe" in
and why?

"What's the use of tryin'?
All you get is pain."
"I'm in love, I'm a believer."
How are these two opposite
emotions echoed in "Alfie"?

What's the advantage or disadvantage in "Sittin on a fence"?

Would you be one of those who say he "has no sense"?

Do you think that "I've been very hard to please; and I don't know wrong from right," has forced him to be a fence-sitter?

Do you agree getting married is just a thing to do?

"But you go out and you don't come back at night." Is running out the only escape from a wrong choice?

Does love require courage to be hurt?

Compare this song with the attitudes concerning love and sex expressed in the Rolling Stones' "Let's Spend the Night Together."

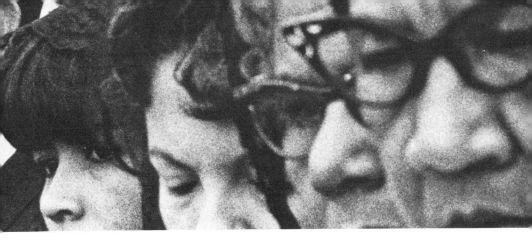

SITTIN' ON A FENCE by Mick Jagger and Keith Richard (Rolling Stones)

"Sittin' on a Fence" by the Rolling Stones describes a young man seeking meaning in life. Confused and unsure he questions the purpose of marriage and the sincerity of love. In the midst of aimlessness he decides on indecision.

Since I was young, I've been very hard to please;
And I don't know wrong from right.
But there is one thing I could never understand—
Some of the sick things that a girl does to a man.

Refrain:
I'm just sitting on a fence; you can say
I got no sense; trying to make up my mind
really is too hard to find,
So I'm sittin' on a fence.

All of my friends from school grew up and
settled down and they mortgaged up their lives.
One thing that's not said too much, but
I think it's true, they just get married
'cause there's nothing else to do.

Refrain:

The day can come when you get old—sick and tired
of life; you just never realize;
maybe the choice you made wasn't really right,
but you go out and you don't come back at night.

Refrain:

GEORGY GIRL *by T. Springfield and J. Dale* (*The Seekers*)

Georgy Girl wears a mask. Lonely, but she doesn't seem lonely. Scared but nobody knows. Searching, but she won't admit it.

It is easy to be a "Georgy Girl," and not show our true emotions; but whatever others think, we ourselves will never be happy or confident. We can only be content with ourselves if we are open and natural. This is dangerous, for we may be hurt. But if we run away from reality, we can never be content.

Would you recognize a Georgy Girl?

" . . . is it the clothes you wear?" Does advertising teach us to measure love by the "clothes you wear"?

"You're always window shopping but never stopping to buy." Does this suggest anything about personal involvement?

How do you think Georgy Girl has run away from reality?

"It's time for jumping down from the shelf." What "shelf"?

What would be the difference if there were "a new Georgy Girl"?

Does the mood of the music fit the lyrics of "Georgy Girl"?

IF I FELL *by Lennon and McCartney* (*Beatles*)

"If I Fell" by the Beatles voices the frustration of being hurt in love. Out of his past sorrow comes a new reason for finding a girl.

If I fell in love with you, would you promise to be true,
and help me understand 'cause I've been in love before and
I found that love was more than just holding hands.

If I give my heart to you, I must be sure from the very
start that you would love me more than her.

If I trust in you, oh please, don't run and hide.
If I love you too, oh please, don't hurt my pride like her
'cause I couldn't stand the pain and I would be sad if our
new love was in vain.

So I hope you see that I would love to love you
And that she will cry, when she learns we are two,
'cause I couldn't stand the pain and I would be sad if
our new love was in vain.

So I hope you see that I would love to love you
And that she will cry, when she learns we are two.
If I fell in love with you . . .

" . . . I found that love was more than just hold-ing hands. . . . " "What "more" did he discover?

" . . . I must be sure from the very start that you would love me more than her." Does his love look within or towards his new love?

" . . . 'cause I couldn't stand the pain and I would be sad if our new love was in vain." According to the song, when is love "in vain"? Do you agree?

" . . . she will cry when she learns we are two." Does his attitude toward his former love feed his desire for his new love?

What do the phrases "I would love to love" and "I would be sad" say about the strength of his emotion?

Compare the attitude toward love in this song with that in "Within You, Without You."

CRUCIFIXION *by Phil Ochs* (*Jim and Jean, "Pleasures of the Harbor" A&M LP4133*)

Crucifixion is the major work of Phil Ochs. This song concerns our crucifixion today, the recurrent life struggle of everyman. It may be probing the extent of personal sacrifice for others that is the basis of all love. It is the response of "others" that is the greatest tragedy in the song.

And the night comes again to the circle studded sky
The stars settle slowly, in loneliness they lie
Till the universe explodes as a falling star is raised
Planets are paralyzed, the mountains are amazed
But they all glow brighter from the brilliance of the blaze
With the speed of insanity, then he dies

In the green fields a-turning a baby is born
His cries crease the wind and mingle with the morn
An assault upon the order, the changing of the guard
Chosen for a challenge that is hopelessly hard
And the only single sighing is the sighing of the stars
But to the silence of distance they are sworn

Refrain: So dance, dance, dance, teach us to be true
come dance, dance, dance, 'cause we love you

Images of innocence, charge him to go on
But the decadence of history is looking for a pawn
To a nightmare of knowledge he opens up the gate
A blinding revelation is served upon his plate
That beneath the gray mist love is a hurricane of hate
And God help the critic of the dawn

So he stands on the sea and he shouts to the shore
But the louder that he screams, the longer he's ignored
For the wine of oblivion is drunk to the dregs
And the merchants of the masses almost have to be begged
Till the giant is aware that someone's pulling at his leg
And someone is tapping at the door

Refrain:

Then his message gathers meaning and spreads across the land
The rewarding of the fame is the falling of the man
But ignorance is everywhere and people have their way
Success is an enemy to the losers of the day
In the shadows of the churches who knows what they pray
And blood is the language of the band

The Spanish bulls are beaten, the crowd is soon beguiled
The Matador is beautiful, a symphony of style
The excitement is ecstatic, passion places bets
Gracefully he bows to ovations that he gets
But the hands that are applauding are slippery with sweat
And saliva is falling from their smiles

Refrain:

Then the silver flow of life is crushed into a lyre
The gentle soul is ripped apart and tossed into a fire
It's the death of beauty, the victory of night
Truth becomes a tragedy limping from the light
Heavens are horrified, they stagger at the sight
And the cross is trembling with desire

They say they can't believe it, it's a sacrilege of shame
Now who would want to hurt such a hero of the game
But you know I predicted it, I knew he had to fall
How did it happen? I hope his suffering was small
Tell me every detail, I've got to know it all
And do you have a picture of the pain

Refrain:

Time takes a toll and the memory fades
But his glory is glowing in the magic that he made
Reality is ruined, there's nothing more to fear
The drama is distorted to what they want to hear
Swimming in their sorrow, in the twisting of a tear
As they wait for the new thrill parade

The eyes of the rebel have been branded by the blind
To the safety of sterility the threat has been refined
The child was created, to the slaughterhouse he's led
So good to be alive when the eulogies are read
The climax of emotion, the worship of the dead
As the cycle of sacrifice unwinds

Refrain:

Repeat verse one

The hero is characterized as standing on the sea (verse 4) and in the bull arena (verse 6). In both these cases, what is his position compared to the mass of men? What do the crowds on the shore and in the grandstand do as he shouts to them and fights the bull?

In the refrain the hero is commanded to "dance," "cause we love you." Is this love of the people authentic?

In response to the "tragedy" in verse 7 "they" say "they can't believe it, it's a sacrilege of shame, now who would want to hurt such a hero of the game, but you know I predicted it, I knew he had to fall . . ."

Would there be parallel responses in our times, in our day-to-day life?

What seems to be the meaning of "the cross is trembling with desire"? (verse 7)

"The drama is distorted to what they want to hear" (verse 9). What is the drama?

"To the safety of sterility the threat has been refined" (verse 10). Who is this threat?

The poet reinforces his ending line "The cycle of sacrifice unwinds" by repeating the first stanza. What is the deeper reflection of this artistic touch?

"Greater love than this no man has than to lay down his life . . ." Christ freely laid down his life that men may live more fully. Do you agree with the introduction that "Crucifixion" probes personal sacrifice for others that is the basis of all love?

What feeling does the sound of the song give you?

GOD IS LOVE by C. J. Rivers (C. J. Rivers)

God is love, and he who abides in love abides in God
and God in him
The love of Christ has gathered us together.
Let us rejoice in Him and be glad.

By this shall all know that we are His disciples,
If we have love one for another.

Owe no man anything except to love one another.
For he who loves his neighbor will fulfill the whole law.

The cup of blessing, which we bless,
Is it not fellowship in the Blood of Christ?

The Bread which we break,
Is it not fellowship in the body of Christ?

This is the Bread that came down from heaven;
He who eats this bread shall live forever.

Paul wrote:
"The love of Christ leaves us no choice, when once we have
reached the conclusion that one man died for all and
therefore all mankind has died. His purpose in dying for all
was that men, while still in life, should cease to live
for themselves and should live for him who for their sake died
and was raised to life. With us therefore worldly standards
have ceased to count in our estimate of any man. . . .
When anyone is united to Christ, there is a new world; the old
order has gone, and a new order has already begun."
(2C 5. 14–18)

Have the songs of love helped you to live this "new order"?

Appendix

*1 I Am A Rock (Simon and Garfunkel)—one person's reaction
to friendship*

2 It Ain't Me Babe (The Turtles)—love asks too much

3 Norwegian Wood (Beatles)—frustrations of "sex for kicks"

4 Light My Fire (Doors)—immediate satisfaction

*5 Red Rubber Ball (Seekers)—"stolen moments of your time
were all you had to give"*

*6 Pictures of Lily (Kinks)—"a little something to solve your
boyhood problem"*

7 For Emily (Simon and Garfunkel)—search for true love

*8 Kathy's Song (Simon and Garfunkel)—"the only truth I know
is you"*

9 Lady Jane (Rolling Stones)—marriage of convenience

10 Suzanne (Judy Collins)—the answer to "Eleanor Rigby"

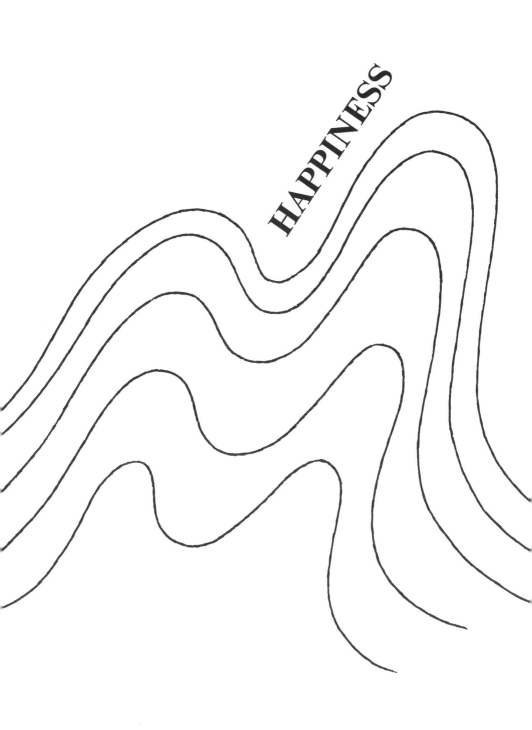

Smiling Faces I Can See

What makes you happy?
A glass of Vodka?
The thrill of wind in your face as you speed
down a highway?
A lover's words to ease your mind?
A twenty dollar bill to make life a groove?
Friday afternoon?
Exhaling the manliness of a Marlboro?
A deal completed at the neighborhood Matthew & Son?
Getting into a good college?
Another glass of Vodka? . . .
Is it true blondes have more fun?

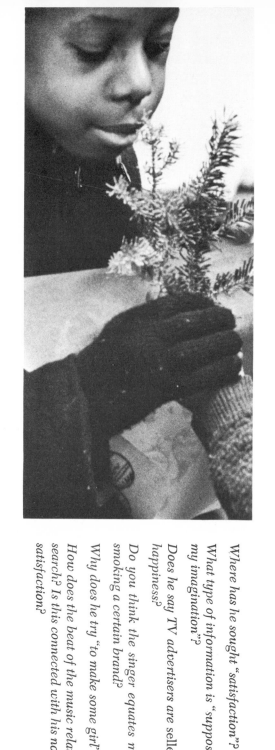

Where has he sought "satisfaction"?

What type of information is "supposed to fire my imagination"?

Does he say TV advertisers are sellers of false happiness?

Do you think the singer equates manliness with smoking a certain brand?

Why does he try "to make some girl"?

How does the beat of the music relate to his search? Is this connected with his not finding satisfaction?

(I CAN'T GET NO) SATISFACTION *by Mick Jagger and Keith Richard*

TV and radio tell us how to join the "in crowd." Imitating heroes and buying products is our instant expressway to happiness. The beat goes on but Mick "can't get no satisfaction."

I can't get no satisfaction,
I can't get no satisfaction,
'Cause I try and I try and I try and I try.
I can't get no, I can't get no,
When I'm drivin' in my car,—
And that man comes on the radio;
And he's tellin' me more and more—
about some useless information,
Supposed to fire my imagination.
I can't get no, Oh, no, no, no,
Hey, hey, hey,—that's what I say.

I can't get no satisfaction,
I can't get no satisfaction,
'Cause I try and I try, and I try and I try.
I can't get no, I can't get no,
When I'm watchin' my T.V.—
And that man comes on to tell me;
How white my shirts can be,
Well, he can't be a man,
'cause he doesn't smoke the same cigarettes as me.
I can't get no, Oh, no, no, no,
Hey, hey, hey,—that's what I say.

I can't get no satisfaction,
I can't get no satisfaction,
'cause I try and I try and I try and I try.
I can't get no, I can't get no,
When I'm ridin' 'round the world,
And I'm doin' this and I'm signin' that;
And I'm tryin' to make some girl.
Who tells me, baby, better come back later next week,
'cause you see I'm on a losing streak.
I can't get no, Oh, no, no, no,
Hey, hey, hey,—that's what I say.

I can't get no, I can't get no,
I can't get no satisfaction,
No satisfaction, No satisfaction, No satisfaction.

"All the things they said were wrong are what I want to be." Is this a common experience of youth growing up?

Do you agree with the comment that looks are shrugged off by teenagers as "irrelativity"?

"I'm not searching for a reason to enjoy myself." Does reasoning enter into enjoyment?

In this day of our affluent society the impression is that you can buy happiness. Does this atmosphere effect our sense of values?

Does the song equate girls and cars?

What is the meaning of the title?

OVER UNDER SIDEWAYS DOWN *by Chris Dreja, Keith Relf,*
Geoff Beck, James McCarty and Paul Samwell-Smith
(The Yardbirds)

Most any guy can get what he wants when he needs it. Why
should he be bothered about what happens when he is finished
with it?

Cars and girls are easy come by in this day and age
Laughing, joking, drinking, smoking till I've spent my wage
When I was young people spoke of immorality
All the things they said were wrong are what I want to be

Refrain:
Over under sideways down—
Backwards forwards square and round
Over under sideways down—
Backwards forwards square and round
When will it end—when will it end
Hey, hey, hey, hey, hey.

I find comment 'bout my looks irrelativity
Think I'll go and have some fun 'cos it's all for free
I'm not searching for a reason to enjoy myself
Seems it's better done than argued with somebody else

Refrain:

SATISFIED MIND *by Rhodes and Hayes* (*Joan Baez*)

The beautiful people mainline money for happiness. But the same rain falls on the rich and poor alike. This song examines the value of money in our lives.

How many times have you heard someone say
If I had his money I'd do things my way
How little they know, it's so hard to find
One rich man in a hundred with a satisfied mind.

Once I was wadding in fortune and fame
Everything I could dream of to get a start in life's game
And then suddenly it happened I lost every dime
But I'm richer by far with a satisfied mind.

No money can buy back your youth when you're old
Or a friend when you're lonely or a love that's grown cold
And the world's richest man is a pauper at times
Compared to the man with a satisfied mind.

When my life is over and time has run out
My friends and my loved ones, I'll leave there's no doubt
But there's one thing for certain when it comes my time
I'll leave this world with a satisfied mind.

Do you agree if you had money you could do things your way?

"I'm richer by far with a satisfied mind"
Why is he satisfied?

Does life in America today make you believe that you can "buy" youth and friends?

How would you advise a person to live so that he could say "I'll leave this world with a satisfied mind."?

In Matthew 5:2–10, Christ calls a person "happy" who lives according to the Beatitudes. Do you think this is a "put on" for a happy life in the modern world?

AS TEARS GO BY *by Mick Jagger, Keith Richard, and Andrew Loog Oldham* (*Rolling Stones*)

A lonely person on a park bench. Children playing all around. Rain flowing by. The past and the present. Through the mist the dim light of the future:

It is the evening of the day
I sit and watch the children play
Smiling faces I can see; but not for me
I sit and watch as tears go by.

My riches can't buy everything
I want to hear the children sing
All I hear is the sound of rain; falling on the ground
I sit and watch as tears go by.

It is the evening of the day
I sit and watch the children play
Doing things I used to do
Thinking of you
I sit and watch as tears go by.

Explain the importance of "It is the evening of the day."

a) How old do you think the singer is?
b) What has this person missed in life?

"My riches can't buy everything."
"And the people who gain the world and lose their soul."
(Within You, Without You)

Compare these two attitudes.

What are the signs of hope in the song?

What is suggested by "All I hear is the sound of rain falling on the ground."?

"You're holding me down, turning me 'round
Filling me up with your rules."
What does this tell us about his attitude in the past?

What is "getting better"?

What "word" turned him on toward life?

"You gave me the word I finally heard
I'm doing the best that I can."
Can one such experience bring about a complete change in a person's life?

GETTING BETTER *by Lennon and McCartney (Beatles)*

There comes a time when playing the game won't satisfy your mind. You find you need someone.

It's getting better all the time
I used to get mad at my school
The teachers that taught me weren't cool
You're holding me down, turning me 'round
Filling me up with your rules.
I've got to admit it's getting better
A little better all the time
I have to admit it's getting better
It's getting better since you've been mine.
Me used to be a angry man
Me hiding me head in the sand
You gave me the word I finally heard
I'm doing the best that I can.
I've got to admit it's getting better
I used to be cruel to my woman
I beat her and kept her apart from the things that she loved
Man I was mean but I'm changing my scene
And I'm doing the best that I can.
I admit it's getting better
A little better all the time
Yes I admit it's getting better
It's getting better since you've been mine.

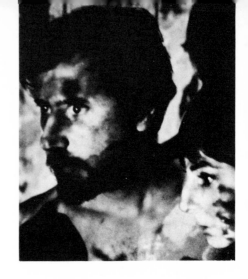

MOTHER'S LITTLE HELPER
by Mick Jagger and Keith Richards (Rolling Stones)

With today's wonders of pharmacy, man has learned to chemically ease his mind. He has developed sophisticated escapes.

What a drag it is getting old
Kids are different today
I hear every mother say
Mother needs something today
to calm her down
And though she's not really ill
There's a little yellow pill.

She goes running for the shelter
of her mother's little helper
And it helps her on her way
Gets her through her busy day.

Things are different today
I hear every mother say
Cooking breakfast for her husband
Just a drag
So she buys an instant cake
And she buys a frozen steak.

And goes running for the shelter
of her mother's little helper
And it helps her on her way
Gets her through her busy day.

Doctor please some more of these
Outside the door she took four more
What a drag it is getting old.

They're just not the same today
I hear every mother say
They just don't appreciate that you get tired
They're so hard to satisfy
You can tranquilize your mind
So go running for the shelter
of your mother's little helper
And they help you through the night
Help to minimize your plight.

Doctor please some more of these
Outside the door she took four more
What a drag it is getting old

Life is much too hard today
I hear every mother say
The pursuit of happiness just seems a bore;
And if you take more of those
You will get an overdose
No more running for the shelter
of your mother's little helper.
They just helped you on your way
to your busy dying day.

Why does she rely on these pills so heavily?

What type of shelter do the pills provide for her?

After the initial escape provided by the pill what does the shelter become?

What is the ultimate escape according to the song?

Is this similar to the escapism of youth who take narcotics and such drugs as marijuana and LSD?

"She taught them all about sex."
Did she really?

"You've got your hang-ups,
it's none of my fault . . . ."
Would you agree?

Mrs. McKenzie's "in a frenzy for
her children to leave so she
can be free." How free do you
think she will be?

"She being more of a friend than
a mother, kept them in her freedom."

"I'm only your mother.
I only work here,
please don't bother me."

"'cause mother's always right."

How true a picture
do you think these lines paint
of a real mother?

Is it a drag "to be wanted"?

Do you teach yourself to be free?
How?

How would you try to help
someone who is "wrapped up in
the twine of the psycho blues"?

MRS. McKENZIE *by Janis Ian* (*Janis Ian*)

She taught them all about sex and other little girls,
Encouraging them to go out among friends and spread the word,
And going from one little game to another,
She being more of a friend than a mother,
Kept them in her freedom.

Refrain
Ah, look, at her, Lady McKenzie, she's in a frenzy
For her children to leave so she can be free.
What a drag it must be feeling wanted!

She said, "If you've got a problem, I'm not here to help you,
You've got your hang-ups, it's none of my fault, pull yourself thru.
Ah, you say you need me, I'm only your mother.
I only work here, please don't bother me.
Teach yourself to be free.

Refrain

I tried to help her, to tell her they wouldn't be what she'd like
                them to
You can't fix your mind if it's wrapped up in the twine of the
                psycho blues
She just said, "Get out, 'cause mother's always right
In a logical world, age means might."
Yeah, and if you're raped chalk it up to experience.

Refrain

Describe the man's happiness as presented in the verses.

Why then does he want to "go home . . . and start over"?

Would he be able to find happiness without "a little bottle of wine"?

What are the sources of this double contradiction in his life?

Can a person absorbed in a "bottle of wine" help himself?

Why do young people turn to alcohol with almost passionate frenzy? A sixteen-year-old girl summed up the situation: "After you have graduated from high school the only way to have fun is to get smashed." A young man described it, "To kill the pain." Would you agree with these attitudes? Why do teenagers drink?

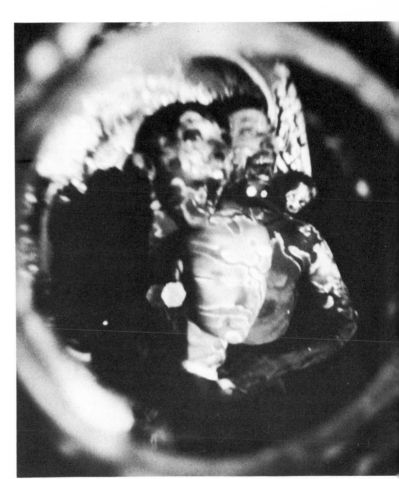

BOTTLE OF WINE *by Tom Paxton* (*Tom Paxton*)

Liquor means different things to different people. For most a simple pleasure; for some teenagers, kicks on a Friday night; for the frustrated businessman, a way out at seven; for the winos on the Bowery, a way of life.

Refrain:
Bottle of wine, fruit of the vine
When you gonna let me get sober
Let me alone, let me go home
Let me go back and start over

Ramblin' around this dirty old town
Singin' for nickles and dimes
Times getting rough, I ain't got enough
To buy a bottle of wine

Refrain:

Little hotel, older than hell
Cold as the dark in the mine
Blankets so thin, I lie there and grin
I got a little bottle of wine

Refrain:

Preacher will preach, teacher will teach
The miner will dig in the mine
I'll ride the roads, trusting in God
Huggin' my bottle of wine

Refrain:

Pain in my head, bugs in my bed
Pants so old that they shine
Out on the street tell the people I meet
Buy a little bottle of wine

Refrain:

Appendix

1 Like a Rolling Stone (Bob Dylan)—what's left when the money's gone

2 Yesterday (Beatles)—memories of love

3 Cod'ine (Buffy Sainte-Marie)—escape through a drug proves no exit

4 Hollis Brown (Bob Dylan)—suicide as an escape from poverty

5 Pack Up Your Sorrows (Judy Collins)—facing life

6 Feelin' Groovy (Simon and Garfunkel)—school's out—you passed. You don't start work for a week. The sun shines on you inside.

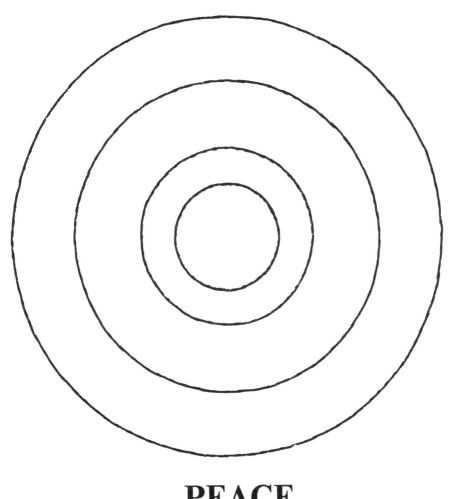

PEACE

When Will They Ever Learn?

As never before total destruction menaces mankind. Planes of superpowers stand on alert loaded with twenty megaton bombs. In the southern hemisphere new nationalisms rise in countries plagued by over-population, hunger, poverty and illiteracy. Across redrawn battle-lines men eye enemies of equally firm dedication to a self-made concept of right.

Yesterday a high-school senior balanced equations, listening to protest songs, taking his girl to the movies. Today he laces up his combat boots and the only sound he hears is the distant thud of guns.

LAST NIGHT I HAD THE STRANGEST DREAM *Words and Music by Ed McCurdy (Pete Seeger)*

Man, the eternal optimist, has always yearned for a day when war would be no more. Ed McCurdy has lyricized our hopes of universal peace in "Last Night I Had the Strangest Dream." As in the Acts of the Apostles "our old men see visions, our young men dream dreams." Man the dreamer, however, is menaced by man the warrior. The challenge is to reconcile the rhetoric of dreamers and the reality of survival.

Last night I had the strangest dream I never dreamed before
I dreamed the world had all agreed to put an end to war
I dreamed I saw a mighty room, and the room was filled with
   men
And the papers they were signing said they'd never fight again.

And when the papers were all signed And a million copies made
They all joined hands and bowed their heads And grateful
   prayers were prayed
And the people in the streets below Were dancing 'round and
   'round
And guns and swords and uniforms Were scattered on the ground

Repeat verse one

Describe your emotions as the song was being played.

Does recent history suggest that this strange dream can become reality?

How can the dream become fact? What happens if it does not?

President Lyndon Johnson met with Premier Kosygin of Russia in June of 1967. The two leaders pledged friendship and peace to each other's country. Do you think such meetings are a way to fulfill "the strangest dream"?

Pope Paul addressed the people of the world at the United Nations in 1965: "Listen to the words of the great departed John Kennedy, who proclaimed four years ago, 'Mankind must put an end to war or war will put an end to mankind.' Many words are not needed to proclaim the loftiest aim of your institution. It suffices to remember that the blood of millions of men, that numberless and unheard of sufferings, useless slaughter and frightful ruin are the sanction of the pact which unites you, with an oath which must change the history of the future world: No more war, war never again!" Are his words merely the madness of a dreamer?

Why is the phrase "Eastern world" so relevant?

"You're old enough to kill but not for votin'"

What difference would it make if youth could vote? Is the present situation hypocritical?

"You don't believe in war, but what's that gun you're totin'"

What is the alternative to carrying a gun?

Christian Americans set themselves in their moral superiority to the Communists. What lines in the song attack this?

How does the lament "over and over and over again" intensify the tragedy of war? (How does this resemble the Universal Soldier and Where Have All the Flowers Gone?)

Can't you feel the fears I'm feelin' today?

"When human respect is disintegratin'" Is the problem isolated in any one country or social issue?

What do you think the heavy beat of the song is trying to say?

EVE OF DESTRUCTION *by P. F. Sloan* (*Barry McGuire*)

Protest songs against war rarely reach the level of frenzy and urgency of Eve of Destruction. *The writer cries out to a world beneath the specter of an H-bomb. Uniting the theme of war and man's inhumanity to man, the song warns of a once-again rapidly approaching disaster—physical, spiritual, and, this time, final.*

The Eastern world, it is explodin'
Violence flarin', bullets loadin'
You're old enough to kill but not for votin'
You don't believe in war, but what's that gun you're totin'
And even the Jordan River has bodies floatin'

Refrain:
But you tell me, over and over and over again, my friend,
Ah, you don't believe we're on the eve of destruction

Don't you understand what I'm tryin' to say
Can't you feel the fears I'm feelin' today
If the button pushed, there's no running away
There'll be no one to save with the world in a grave
Take a look around you, boy, it's bound to scare you, boy

Refrain:

Yeh, my blood's so mad feels like coagulatin'
I'm sittin' here just contemplatin'
I can't twist the truth it knows no regulatin'
Handful of Senators don't pass legislation
And marches alone can't bring integration
When human respect is disintegratin'
This whole crazy world is just too frustratin'

Refrain:

Think of all the hate there is in Red China
Then take a look around to Selma, Alabama
You may leave here for four days in space
But when you return it's the same old place
The pounding of drums, the pride and disgrace
You can bury your dead but don't leave a trace
Hate your next door neighbor but don't forget to say grace.

Refrain:

113

What is the tragedy of the phrase "heavenly sound"?

Bob Dylan wrote the song "A Hard Rain's A-Gonna Fall" at the time of the Cuban missile crisis in 1962. What rain is the subject of these two songs? What policy of our government is being criticized?

Can anything survive the onslaught of the rain?

What is the irony in the fact that rain brings disaster? How is this reflected by the use of our technology?

WHAT HAVE THEY DONE TO THE RAIN? *Malvina Reynolds*
(*Joan Baez*)

"This is the gentlest protest song I know. It doesn't protest gently, but it sounds gentle."   *Joan Baez*

Just a little rain falling all around,
The grass lifts its head to the heavenly sound,
Just a little rain, just a little rain,
What have they done to the rain?

Just a little boy standing in the rain,
The gentle rain that falls for years,
And the grass is gone, the boy disappears,
And rain keeps falling like helpless tears,
And what have they done to the rain?

Just a little breeze out of the sky,
The leaves nod their heads as the breeze blows by,
Just a little breeze with some smoke in its eye,
What have they done to the rain?

Repeat verse 2

115

THE UNIVERSAL SOLDIER *by Buffy Sainte-Marie* (*Buffy Sainte-Marie*)

"The Universal Soldier" of Buffy Sainte-Marie strongly condemns individual participation in war. It hurls a challenge across the scope of time and through the manifold refinements of "the cause" at every man who has taken up a gun.

He's five foot two and he's six feet four
He fights with missiles and with spears
He's all of thirty one and he's only seventeen
He's been a soldier for a thousand years
He's a Catholic, a Hindu, an atheist, a Jane
a Buddhist, and a Baptist and a Jew
And he knows he shouldn't kill
And he knows he always will
Kill you for me my friend and me for you
And he's fighting for Canada, he's fighting for France
He's fighting for the U.S.A.
And he's fighting for the Russians and he's fighting for Japan
And he thinks we'll put an end to war that way
And he's fighting for democracy, He's fighting for the Reds
He says it's for the peace of all
He's the one who must decide who's to live and who's to die
And he never sees the writing on the wall
But without him how would Hitler have condemned him at
               Dachau
Without him Caesar would have stood alone
He's the one who gives his body as a weapon of the war
And without him all this killing can't go on
He's the Universal Soldier and he really is to blame
His orders come from far away no more
They come from him and you and me and brothers can't you see
This is not the way to put an end to war.

How do you get universal soldiers on opposite sides of the battle line to come to peace conferences when both are convinced that they are right and God is on their side?

"And he knows he shouldn't kill
  And he knows he always will"
Why does he know he shouldn't kill?

"And he never sees the writing on the wall"
What does the writing on the wall mean?

Who is the "Universal Soldier" today?
Can he put an end to war?

MASTERS OF WAR *by Bob Dylan* (*Bob Dylan*)

"Masters of War" is a bitter attack by Bob Dylan upon those who manufacture weaponry for profit. Modern economies have become more and more dependent upon government purchasers of war materials, produced for gain and providing more employment for the labor force. Eventually the production lines achieve such importance that wars or imaginary threats are manufactured to meet their supply. The voice of the idealist pervades the stock exchange, asking whether this aspect of war or weaponry itself is moral.

You who hide behind walls,
and who hide behind desks.
Does this apply only to weapons'
manufacturers? How do others
profit from the danger of war?

Do you think it is valid to deny
youth a voice because of
inexperience?

You want me to believe that a
world can be gained.
Can a world war be won?

Is it true that the worse fear
brought about by war is the fear
to bring children into the world?

Which attitude is better—that of
the protester or that of the
"Masters of War"?
Which strengthens the peace
of the world?

"Whatever be the case with this
method of deterence, men
should be convinced that the
arms race in which so many
countries are engaged is not a
safe way to preserve a steady
peace. Nor is the so-called
balance resulting from this race
a sure and authentic peace.
Rather than being eliminated
thereby, the causes of war
threaten to grow stronger."
From The Church in the Modern
World, *ch. 5, section 1*
"Avoidance of War."

Is the manufacture of weaponry
(or use of it), especially that
used against non-combatants,
moral?

119

I marched to the battle of New Orleans
At the end of the early British War
The young land started growin', the young blood started flowin'
But I ain't marchin' anymore

For I killed my share of Indians
At a thousand different fights
I was there at the Little Big Horn
I heard the men lyin', I saw many boys dyin'
But I ain't marchin' anymore

Refrain:
It's always the old who lead us to war
It's always the young who fall
Now look at what we've won with saber and a gun
Tell me is it worth it all?

For I stole California from the Mexican lands
Fought in the bloody civil war
Yes I've even killed my brothers and so many others
But I ain't marchin' anymore

For I marched to the battle of the German trench
In a war that was bound to end all war
Oh I must have killed a million men
And now they want me back again
But I ain't marchin' anymore

Refrain:

For I flew the final mission in the Japanese sky
Set off the mighty mushroom roar
When I saw the cities burnin' I knew that I was learnin'
That I ain't marchin' anymore

Now the labor leaders scream
When they close the missile plants
And United Fruit cries at the Cuban shore
Call it peace or call it treason
Call it love or call it reason
But I ain't marchin' anymore

Refrain:

I AIN'T MARCHIN' ANYMORE *by Phil Ochs* (*Phil Ochs*)

A declaration of conscience by just one of the universal and timeless soldiers of history. Like "The Universal Soldier," however, this song seemingly ignores the arguments for self defense and the reasons against pacifism.

In any sense can it be said that the soldiers in this song and in "The Universal Soldier" are the same?

It has been suggested that the draft age be changed from between 18 and 26 to between 42 and 50. What echoes this in "I Ain't Marchin' Anymore"?

"Call it peace or call it treason
Call it love or call it reason"
Does he equate treason with peace, love or reason? What demands does this make on a person?

What have we won with a saber and a gun?

BLOWIN' IN THE WIND *by Bob Dylan (Peter, Paul, and Mary)*

Blowin' in the Wind *has become the hymn of peace throughout the world. It summarizes in nine brief questions the infinitude of human inhumanity. Although the sophisticated may call the song simplistic, we feel it penetrates history with clear perception. The answer blowin' in the wind goes unheard by apathetic man.*

"The answer is blowin' in the wind."
Give your interpretation of this mysterious phrase.

Throughout the song lines on war are paralleled by lines on individual dignity. Explain the connection.

What is the mountain referred to in the third verse?

Why would someone turn his head and pretend that he doesn't see? Is this intentional?

Compare the message of the song with the peace formula of Pope Paul VI: "To wage war on misery and to struggle against injustice is to promote along with improved conditions, the human and spiritual progress in all men, and therefore is a common good of humanity. Peace cannot be limited to a mere absence of war the result of an ever precarious balance of forces. No peace is something that is built up day after day, in the pursuit of an order intended by God which implies a more perfect form of justice among men."
*from—*Populorum Progressio: *Development is the New Name for Peace*

Is the song optimistic or pessimistic?

Appendix

1 The Great Mandella (Peter, Paul, and Mary)—just playing the game

2 Cruel War (Peter, Paul, and Mary)—love weathers war

3 Scarborough Fair/Canticle (Simon and Garfunkel)—visions of war in a sprinkling of leaves

4 Twenty Tons of TNT (Pete Seeger)—three billion humans and sixty billion tons of bombs

5 The Dove (Judy Collins)—a soldier's goodbye to his lover

6 Where Have All the Flowers Gone? (Peter, Paul, and Mary)— "Those who forget history are bound to repeat it."

7 The Sun Is Burning (Simon and Garfunkel)—on any day, at any time, the Bomb

8 With God on Our Side (Bob Dylan)—we are the good guys of the world

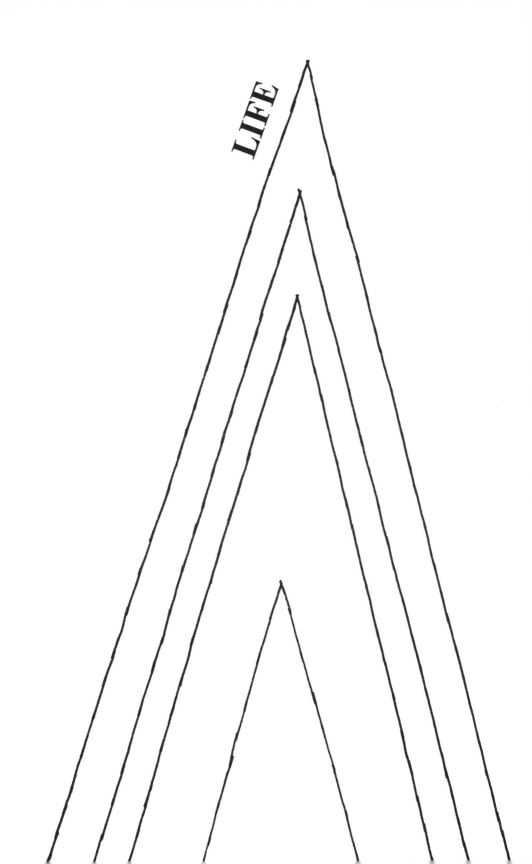

One Last Cup of Wine

    Through the crowds, through the cars speeding by, through the images flowing through our minds we look for permanence. Life vanishes in the mad flux of the city. We wake up and in a moment it is nightfall. We enter high school and too soon it's college. We rush to catch our breath at some goal we never reach. Perhaps we retreat into the shadows of dream, unable to make reality sane.

    Our music echoes the chaos of our time. We hear voices confused and agonized and voices calm and certain. We hear above all the pulse beat of modern life.

FLOWERS NEVER BEND WITH THE RAINFALL *by P. Simon (Simon and Garfunkel)*

Sometimes it happens. Things aren't going too bad—just routine. Maybe you look at the stars on a clear night, and maybe you haven't really looked at anything. Maybe it's something as sacred as a beautiful chapel or maybe it's something as sickening as a toothpaste commercial that promises to give your mouth sex appeal. But there you are, suddenly wondering where you really are, thinking about Things, wondering if they all add up. It doesn't happen often and not for long. In a few minutes you're back, pretending your life will never end. But it will, you'll see, and flowers do really bend with the rainfall.

*Why does he hide behind
the shield of his illusion?*

*What does it mean to be blinded by the light of
God? By the light of truth? By the right?*

Is it ordinary to pretend? Is it expected?

Why does his fantasy become his reality?

*He does not know what is real. Nor can he touch
what he feels. Do you know what is real?*

*He is what he must be and faces the future.
What makes him what he is?*

Does he face the future optimistically?

FIVE O'CLOCK WORLD *by Allen Reynolds* (*Vogues*)

Modern America has become a land regulated by the hours 9 through 5. While hippies revolt against dehumanization, others seek to put meaning into the rat race. Human values must win out even within the typewriter jungle.

Up every morning just to keep my job
I gotta find my way through the hustling mob,
Sounds of the city pounding in my brain
While another day goes down the drain.

But it's a five o'clock world when the whistle blows
No one owns a piece of my time.
And there's a five o'clock me inside my clothes
Thinking that the world looks fine.

Trading my time for the pay I get
Living on the money that I ain't made yet.
Gotta keep goin', gotta make my way
But I live for the end of the day.

But it's a five o'clock world when the whistle blows,
And no one owns a piece of my time.
And there's a long haired girl who waits, I know,
To ease my troubled mind.

In the shelter of her arms everything's O.K.
She talks and the world goes slipping away,
And I know a reason I can still go on
When every other reason is gone.

In my five o'clock world she waits for me,
Nothing else matters at all.
'cause every time my baby smiles at me,
I know it's all worthwhile.

What is the importance of the girl in his life?

Would you want to be part of the five o'clock world?

What value does he place on his work?

Is there any alternative to a "five o'clock world"?

How can the five o'clock world become a Christian world?

The singer's voice almost cracks with despair as he sings until the words "I'd love to turn you on." Why?

Why is the man who committed suicide described as lucky?

Why does the singer have to laugh at the sad news?

"I'd love to turn you on" the singer says, just prior to a deafening crescendo of noise. It might be similar to a marijuana buzz. Does this line refer to drugs?

Do you think that the Beatles would think your answer to the fourth question important?

What is the significance of the "crowd of people"?

"And its conclusion though magnificent, seems to represent a negation of self. The song ends on one low note that is sustained for forty seconds. Having achieved the absolute peace of nullification, the narrator is beyond melancholy. But there is something brooding and irrevocable about his calm. It sounds like destruction." The New York Times, June 18, 1967. Do you agree with this interpretation?

A DAY IN THE LIFE *by Lennon and McCartney (Beatles)*

"A Day in the Life" is, according to The New York Times, *a major accomplishment, obviously describing "the banality of modern life." Ultimately, says* The Times, *it is the alleged use of drugs by the Beatles which will prevent this song from reaching the mass audience. In its conclusion, a forty second note suggests the nullification of self.*

I read the news today oh boy
About a lucky man who made the grade
And though the news was rather sad
Well I just had to laugh
I saw the photograph.
He blew his mind out in a car
He didn't notice that the lights had changed
A crowd of people stood and stared
They'd seen his face before
Nobody was really sure
If he was from the House of Lords.
I saw a film today oh boy
The English army had just won the war
A crowd of people turned away
But I just had to look
Having read the book.
I'd love to turn you on
Woke up, fell out of bed,
Dragged a comb across my head
Found my way downstairs and drank a cup,
And looking up I noticed that I was late.
Found my coat and grabbed my hat
Made the bus in seconds flat
Found my way upstairs and had a smoke,
Somebody spoke and I went into a dream
I read the news today oh boy
Four thousand holes in Blackburn, Lancashire
And though the holes were rather small
they had to count them all
Now they know how many holes it takes to fill Albert Hall.
I'd love to turn you on

Who are the green leaves
of summer?

Part of the song is a remi-
niscence of youth. Have
you experienced this in
your own personal life?

"Your tears will be
trembling, now we're somewhere else, one last cup
of wine we will pour
And I'll kiss you one
more time and leave you
on the rolling river shore
of changes"
Do you become chained
down to the past? To what
might have been?

Does the song admit there
is anything of permanence
in the world?

CHANGES *by Phil Ochs (Phil Ochs in Concert—Electra Records EKS7310)*

Change and time have been recurrent themes in our literature. Man watches as nature cycles itself on the road of the past, present and future. He must adapt to a world constantly evolving into something new. The songs Changes and Circle Game (next) ask, like the ballad writer of Medieval France, "Where are the snows of yesteryear?"

Sit by my side, come as close as the air, share in a memory
of gray and wander in my words and dream about the pictures I
        play
of changes
Green leaves of summer turn red in the fall, to brown and to
yellow they fade
And then they have to die, trapped within the circle time parade
of changes
Scenes of my young years were warm in my mind, visions of
        shadows that shined
Till one day I returned and found they were victims of the line
of changes
The world spinning madly, it drifts in the dark, and swings
through a hollow of haze
A race around the sun, a journey through a universe of lace
with changes
Moments of magic will grow in the night, all fears of the forest
are gone
But when the morning breaks they're swept away by the golden
drops of dawn
and changes
Passions will part to a strange melody, as fires will sometimes
grow cold
Like petals in the wind, we're puppets to the silver strings of soul
and changes
Your tears will be trembling, now we're somewhere else, one
last cup of wine we will pour
And I'll kiss you one more time and leave you on the rolling
river shore
of changes

THE CIRCLE GAME *by Joni Mitchell* (*Buffy Sainte-Marie*)

Yesterday a child came out to wander, caught a dragonfly
inside a jar
Fearful when the sky was full of thunder, and tearful at the
falling of a star
Then the child moved ten times round the seasons, skated
over ten year frozen streams
Words like "when you're older" must appease him, and promises
of someday make his dreams

Refrain:

The seasons they go round and round and the painted ponies
go up and down
We're captives on the carousel of time, we can't return we
can only look behind from where we came
And go round and round and round in the circle game

Sixteen springs and sixteen summers gone now
cartwheels lost to carwheels through the town
And you tell him, take your time it won't be long now,
till you drag your feet to slow those circles down
So the boy who dreamed "tomorrow" now is twenty,
though his dreams have lost some grandeur coming true
They'll be new dreams, maybe better dreams and plenty,
before the last revolving year is through

Refrain:

"Words like 'when you're older' must appease him,
and promises of someday make his dreams"
Does this end with childhood?

Are we captive on a carousel of time?

"Though his dreams have lost some grandeur coming
true"
Can this be said about all youthful ideals?
Is an end to dreaming a sign of maturity?

"Till you drag your feet to slow those circles down"
At what age does this begin?

Is human life a circle game leading nowhere?

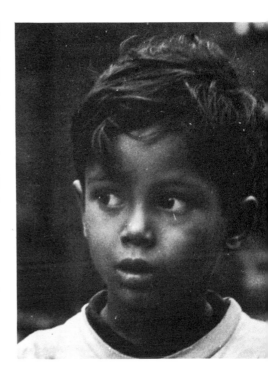

Appendix

1 When I'm Gone (Phil Ochs)—"miles to go before I sleep"

2 Matthew and Son (C. Stevens)—the 8:15 train and 5 P.M. bell

3 Mr. Tambourine Man (Bob Dylan) (The Byrds)—a trip upon a magic swirling ship

4 Turn, Turn, Turn (The Byrds and Judy Collins)—a time for everything under heaven

5 Pastures of Plenty (Woody Guthrie)—working and wandering across America

"One generation passes and another comes, but the world forever stays. The sun rises and the sun goes down; then it presses on to the place where it rises. . . . All speech is labored; there is nothing man can say. The eye is not satisfied with seeing nor is the ear filled with hearing."

Ecclesiastes 1, 4.5.8.

IN SONG

Great rock and folk rock —
an exciting new way of talking
about life and faith by and
for the young in heart.